GOD HAS AN APP FOR THAT

I0158477

Harry Hickerson

Dedication

I would like to dedicate this book to my son, Matthew Bryant Hickerson. Matthew you've inspired this writing. Our journey has given me a new respect for relationships. Without our journey I may have never transitioned into the man I am today. Facing difficulty is not always easy. But having someone looking to and depending on you forces you to embrace it and take it head on. Matthew you have been that for me. I was told once you will have to live the information you know. This is that! I am so grateful for our relationship son. I never want to take that for granted.

I'm excited to see the results of the great things in store for your life. The greatest gift my mother gave me was constantly rehearsing and reminding me who I was and who I would become. Until this day I can still hear her voice and feel her push. Without her intense pursuit for life, I don't show up! My prayer is that this book would be your push and serve as a reminder to you of who you are. I love you son, dad.

Acknowledgements

I give honor, glory and thanks to God for inspiring my heart and mind to write. Thank you for unlocking the author that was inside of me!

Thanks to my beautiful wife Antoinette, for your love, continued support and dedication throughout our life together. My life would not be the same without you by my side.

Thanks to my two awesome daughters Kayla and Nicole. I am proud of both of you. You make being a father the best!

Thanks to my first motivational speaker my Mother Wanda Farris. All your life's lessons, your never quit tenacity and your persistence I carry with me daily. Your sacrifice for our family so that I could be where I am in life today will never be forgotten. Thank you to my father Harry Hickerson Sr. I appreciate every deposit you made in my life.

Thanks to my pastors Edwin and Alma Bamberg. Your teachings and support over the years have been the framework to the life I know and have now. I appreciate your labor of love.

TABLE OF CONTENTS

Introduction

It's December 31st around 1:30pm, I'm at work and I get the call. My wife shares that her water broke and I should get there now. I can't explain the feeling of joy and happiness that rushed through me. We have a ten-year-old daughter at the time. But this is my first birth experience and to top it off it's our first son! I don't remember the drive home to get the bags or the drive to the hospital. All I'm thinking is Lord don't let me miss this one. Fast forward I arrive, my wife and I are so excited, but my son decides to wait to be born on his due date January 1st.

Not only does he wait to be born on his due date, but he's the last of five other babies born that day. Around 3:45pm the miracle happens and it's to this day one of the best moments of my life! The memories I have of my father were from early childhood, a few from my teen years and the rest would be from my latter adult life.

If my son doesn't get much from me the one thing, he and all my children will get is the best father and dad that I can provide.

No knock on my father he did the best out of what he had to offer and I'm so grateful for him. I just want more for my children.

We're in the hospital about to be released to go home for the first time and I'm fast forwarding through Matthew's life, of all the things we'll get to do and experiences to come. Trust me, all of it is nothing but good things.

Not for one second do you imagine anything bad happening or life-threatening taking place.

You know once you see them and hold them there's nothing you wouldn't do for them. But the truth is the timeline of their life is only known by the life giver.

Moving forward through Matthew's childhood, we shared the good, bad and funny of it like most parents. Also, during this period, we have the last edition to our family his sister Nicole. Our hands are full as parents and they are giving us all we can handle. But life takes a turn once Matthew starts school.

His teachers begin to share their concerns with us regarding his progress in school. For us, this was a little shocking and concerning.

He's not new to school he'd been attending daycare for a while and everything was good.

So, after a series of tests and doctors' visits, we get the news Matthew has ADHD. For me this was crushing. One of the responsibilities of a father is protection. It's tough knowing that there are some things you can't protect your children from. It seemed after the diagnosis everything began to come apart at the seam.

Even at his young age, he knew something was going on with him and we could tell the affect it had on him. This was hard on us as parents. We knew things had changed and we needed to come up with a plan to help our son.

For me it took a minute because around the same time, I would find out that I was battling the same thing my son was battling.

At first, I turned a deaf ear to it and went through this prolonged pity party.

But thank God for my village, my wife, my pastors, my psychologist and the word. This was a huge turning point for my son, for me and my family. During this time, I was an active youth leader and looking back at it, I can see clearly how God used it and many other things to pull my son and I out!

God birthed in me a strategy and a mantra that would not only help and save my son and I but whoever would work it.

Little did I know at the time, it would become a movement and a playbook for life. God gave me the answer through a problem. Take out every problem you've put away to hide from the pain of it and start listening for the answer that's in it! Neither my son nor I are where we once were and that's only because we chose to download the app specific for our situation.

I pray Matthew as you and countless others read this playbook that the seasons and transitions of life are successful due to the apps that have been downloaded in this book.

Welcome to God has An App for That.

Chapter One
"I Hope You Get MADD"

In order to use an app and partake of what it has to offer, it requires effort and work. Through effort, you gain a knowing and confidence. Through work, you exercise and build up the areas that need strengthening and stamina.

I've found in my life there were missing apps. I remember being diagnosed and confronted with ADHD; I was heartbroken and lost.

Part of it was I'd been living this way for so long and the thought of having this disorder at this stage of life, the thought of change intimidated me. Your perception is big! I wasn't sure at this stage of life that I wanted to accept it and embrace the change needed to improve and become better.

It wasn't until the doctor said these words," Mr. Hickerson, your son is taking the medication to be better and do better and you're not willing to try!

It was in that moment I decided that I would get MADD and beat this! Not just for me but for my son and all I would ever come in contact with who suffered from this disorder.

I hope as you are reading this that you get MADD! MADD is an acronym for Motivation, Activation to overcome Distractions and Disappointments.

In order to advance in life, there are times and situations that calls for us to get MADD! This disorder with my son was the breaking point. He couldn't express himself at that age, but I could understand his pain, frustration and confusion. I had lived with this scar for years without being able to say anything to anyone and to know my son could possibly go through the same horror shook and awakened something in me.

I didn't get a push to write a book until years later. For two years, I wrestled back and forth internally trying to know how to help myself and my son. Finally, the answer or the App for That was revealed to me! The week had come, and we were preparing to take our teens to a youth conference as we had always done this time of the year. This time I was struggling like I had never struggled before with ADHD.

I was struggling as a husband, a father, a man, and as a youth leader. I'm normally bouncing off the walls for the youth conference, but this time around I just didn't have it. I was having one big pity party. I felt like I had nothing to say or even be a leader at the time because in my eyes I didn't qualify and measure up. I cried out for help like I never had before. The most incredible thing began to happen while away at this youth conference.

God did open heart surgery on me and begin to show me from His word who I was in Him and what I had in Him despite everything that happened to me and the things I was going through.

By the end of the week, not only was I seeing clearly but for the first time in my life, the things that had come to stop me and discourage me had no more power over me. God showed me that week how to get MADD!

At the time, it was given to me in the form of a lesson, but little did I know it would become my mantra, a book and movement! God has an APP for That!

What my son and I were going through was the motivation. That activation came from my seeking and cry out for help! Hitting a wall in life with all the things my hands were on was discouraging.

Those distractions had all my attention until that's all I was consumed with. What I realized is when you experience disappointments if you are not careful past disappointments will become the expectation for anything you attempt or think about attempting. That's where I was docked, right there rehearsing all the failures, mishaps and the pain of them. Thank God for the App He has for That.

When I cried out for help, He downloaded not only what I needed but what would help others to!

If there is something in life that motivates you, find it, embrace it! Activation happens out of an on purpose pursuit to be recused from what has the potential to stop you, distract you and kill you whether that is physical death, mental death or emotional death!

Distractions happens to us all. None of us are exempt from distractions. They are a normal part of life and you must learn to overcome them, or they will overcome you.

Disappointments are necessary for growth and maturity. You are right; they hurt. But so does birthing a child (so I've been told).

The beauty of the baby and who the baby is destined to be would never be known without the sacrifice of the mother who willingly goes through the discomfort of the pregnancy. The transformation her body goes through in preparation to push something out that not only is going to bless the mother but all who encounters the baby is worth it.

Never again look at disappointment and discomfort as hurt and inconvenience but see it as the birth canal to a greater and better life!

When I was in the doctor's office, I couldn't see any of what God was going to do through it all.

Maybe you are reading this and can't see your way either. It's not a bad place to be. Why? Get MADD and watch the transforming power of God change your scene of life from victim to victory. It wasn't just the one thing; it was a sentence being unveiled to me in parts.

It was during this season of life that God was building me. All the different things that were happening was purpose being birthed through the painful situations. God doesn't pursue us the way we think or expect. The pursuit comes in the way of problems. You are a problem solver! You're saying, yeah right, why is my life like this. I didn't think I was either. The problem has a way of unlocking the hidden potential that is lying dormant inside you. I'm telling you it is time to get MADD! Get motivated to change and then activate it.

Then watch the distractions and disappointments begin to change in your favor in life. They may not all go away, but God will give you the grace to stand and fight until your change comes.

I'm living proof of that! So, what's your plan for change? One of the things that helps is finding yourself a role model. Having that accountability is the fuel you'll need especially in the tough times when you want to give up. What does it look like?

Some are in person. Some are over the phone. Some are out of their books and teachings they write. I have a few of them. Some of them we'll never meet. I follow some from afar.

You must find out what works for you. It's going to challenge every fiber of you, but if you are willing to put in the work, you'll be amazed at the results! My son and I are not out of the woods in our situation Yet! But we're not where we once were either.

We've just decided that we are going to beat it and while beating it, we'll help as many people as we can on our way out!

Get MADD! Someone is waiting on your victory. Someone's life is in need of your story. Even if you've been told your life isn't going to amount to anything!

It's a lie! Your life matters and it matters so much that the App Developer gave His son that you and I would have life and have it more abundantly.

Stop rehearsing everything that's wrong and things that are out of place. Download the app, work within the app and use the app to perform the specific tasks life demands. You have the app to overcome. In the app is the pre-installed victory and win you desire. Let the downloading begin.

Chapter Two
"There's a Fixing in the Following"

It's not always easy to have something fixed. Especially when you don't think it's broken or needs fixing. I'm a country boy still to this day and we spent a lot of time fixing things that need and require repairing whether for ourselves or for others. It would seem the principal and process of fixing things should come easy for me in that respect, but it didn't. It was the total opposite.

There are many ways fixing takes place. There's a quick fix, an overnight fix, a gradual fix, a fix it over time just to name a few. The fix I want to talk about is the fixing in the following! Thank God life happens in seasons and not in plays.

One of my favorite biblical characters is Peter. Many times, looking into his life has been like a mirror for me. I'm so thankful for it.

We see a lot of bad plays in Peter's life, but it was through the seasons of his life that continues to encourage readers of his life still today. From our studies, we learn Peter was one of the disciples Jesus kept close to him. Which was something I never had. I wasn't good at allowing others to hold me accountable. I was able to see others thrive and succeed and I knew I had what it takes to succeed but I would come up short time after time.

After a while, whether you admit it or not you think about it and it eats at you and causes frustration and you begin to blame others and situations for your place in life. The reason why was the absence of this principle.

Sometimes the pressure and pursuit of perfection is misleading.

You will experience breakdowns in life, but the process of following can eliminate time-lapse that affects your destiny and your purpose.

When I think of fixing, I think of the Extreme Makeover home shows. The home looks to be stuck and hopeless in one state. Then a group of people who cares enough goes on a journey to transform the home into another state.

Some call that a makeover. I call it a fixing. I'm so thankful for makeovers and fixing. I'm writing and speaking to you because of an Extreme Makeover! Let me first say it's possible. I'm living proof that it's possible. You're proof to! The question is will you embrace it?

I've followed a lot of things in my life time. Some good, some bad, and some I'm still trying to figure out, lol! There are many principles found in following something for the long haul. I would like to focus our attention on a Fixing in the Following.

We can see this in the lives of our servicemen and servicewomen after committing to a branch of service. We can see this in the process of our teens leaving for college and returning years later as young men and young women.

But there are times when you are asked to follow something that you don't believe will lend to you being fixed. Some followings in life are downright scary and it takes discipline and faith colliding to make it work. It would make it ok if you knew everything in the Fixing in the Following process. But it doesn't work that way and some of us spend a life time starting and stopping, waiting for everything to make sense.

I hope you find relief in this, that if you have or maybe you're in the process of a merry go round, you can stop, get off, get your balance and move towards the intended destination.

The uncomfortable fixing. There are some things we know that needs a makeover. Then there are some things that others help us to know we need makeovers for. Know this; the makeover is not solely for you. The big picture is designed to ground you that you may be able to help and ground others. The one wondering thing about the Fixing in the Following, you really can't target or pin when the makeover happens, all you know is that what I use to have I no longer have.

But while you're in it, it doesn't feel that way. One key is to find someone who has successfully experienced the makeover as your role model. It makes achieving the goal doable. Don't allow the ugly things we're embarrassed to share or talk about stop you! We see this in the life of Peter and Jesus. No matter what Peter had going on or how ugly the situation, Jesus encouraged Peter that there was a Fixing in the Following. Even in Peter's rock bottom state, there was a word reminding him of the Fixing in the Following.

I want to encourage you no matter where you find yourself, continue to follow; your strength is connected to it.

Because of a speech impediment and dyslexia, I struggled for years with speaking in public and in front of groups of people which both are a part of what my purpose is in life. Many that knew me said they couldn't tell. But for me, it was tough and frustrating.

There was a lot of negative perception from my own accord and I knew that it wasn't where it should have been, and it nearly shut me down. Thank God my path was connected to, two individuals whose call in life is to help others identify their worth in life, my Pastors Edwin and Alma Bamberg. They are Potential Maximizers. It's amazing now how clear I can see things but going through the Fixing in the Following was tough.

I didn't see and couldn't see at the time all the things I was doing and learning to help me in this extreme makeover. As I shared with you earlier, you don't even know when it happens. Another key is doing it in season, out of season and just being faithful to the instructions given without full understanding.

We live in a nation, a world where no one wants to follow but rather lead.

Because of this, we see the cracks in the foundation that's plaguing our families, our communities and our world.

The extreme makeovers needed must start with us, in our homes. Fathers and sons, mothers and daughters, from one generation to another. No matter what figure it is, spiritual, biological or natural, we must start somewhere to fix what's broken.

My life is the better, my family's life is better because I submitted to a Fixing in the Following.

Matthew, my prayer for you and my grandchildren is that you would be light years ahead of what I was and where I was. There are some natural things you must conquer in order to arrive at your destiny.

Some are in this book, but others you will learn in your pursuit after God. Whether I'm here with you or not you must never abort the process of the Fixing in the Following.

The Peter after Jesus death would have never manifested without the Fixing in the Following. Your Fixing in the Following Potential Conditioners are out there. They are critical for your improvement and advancement in life.

Be open and change your perception about being coached and mentored. Their purpose is not to be your friend and make you feel good.

It's about exposing and strengthening weakness and making you better in those areas.

It's about helping you understand that the only way to bake a cake is to put it in the oven. The heat and the consistency of time in a set place bring forth what was in the mind of the app developer. God uses people to usher you into your destiny. So, if you are looking for another way, you'll just waste time on the game clock of your life.

Chapter Three
"It's Time to do New Math with a New Math Mind"

I didn't do well in school. Not because I wasn't able. No, I didn't focus on it. It's one of the few things I'd wish I could go back and change. If you are reading this playbook encourage someone, push them, push yourself to do well and be well in school. It's very important. The landscape has changed in education.

Though my grades didn't reflect it, I really enjoyed history and debate. If only other classes could have held my attention like these maybe things would have turned out differently.

There will be things in life that don't appeal to you the way things you like do.

It's in those moments and times you must display and demonstrate focus. It would seem as though this is very elementary, and we ought to know this.

There is a landscape where none of this matter and whatever you feel like is accepted. I want to challenge you to think outside the box. I call this doing New Math with a New Math Mind.

Years ago, I was helping my son with his math homework. Even though math wasn't my strength in school, I could help him with this assignment. He and I started the homework and I noticed something immediately.

It was taking him a long time to complete each problem. I looked at his work and said, I see why it is taking you so long. I showed him how I did this type of math when I was in school and he immediately told me that's not how the teacher showed us.

We must do it this way to receive credit for the homework. It's already late I told him let's do it my way so we can finish and go to bed. We finished I felt great I helped my son with his homework, his Mom was happy, no problem Dad to the recuse!

Until the next day, he brought the grade to me and he made a 27, ouch! My wife contacted the teacher and she explained why he received the grade. He could redo the homework, this time he passed it and knocked it out the park.

Where was the error? Me and my methods and my unwillingness to listen! My wife helps our teens with their homework now, lol.

I realized through this situation not only had the way math was done changed, but the way the world functions had changed and if he and my daughters were going to succeed, they would have to do New Math with a New Math Mind. What do I mean by that? When you look at the basic math problem of 2+2=4. There are two things that stand out in this equation, the + and the =. The thing that give forward ability is the +. The plus has the power to move forward and enables ability to the = sign.

We live in a time and moment where everyone and everything wants to be equal or have equality. If you are functioning with an old mindset and old way of doing things, you run the risk of being left behind. No one wants to be left behind. I know firsthand. In one of the most exciting times of a teenager's life, transitioning from Jr. High to High School is the best.

I missed that opportunity because of poor effort and poor grades and unfortunately, I had to repeat the 8th grade.

Oh, sure I wanted to be equal with all my classmates and go to the 9th grade, but I neglected to do all the + that would enable me the ability to move forward.

The greatest lesson my mother could give me was allowing me to repeat the 8th grade.

She could have sent me to summer school just to pass me along, no!

She understood it would pay greater dividends later in my life. Now I help deter others because someone dared to do New Math with a New Math Mind!

Thank you, Momma, my first Potential Conditioner. Your tough unwavering love has been the major contributing fabric in my life, and it has held me down for all these years and continues to wear and stretch in my life!

Nothing troubles and worries a parent like the concern of their children.

With the pressures of living and life, there are seasons that really challenge our families and it's during those tough times and see nothing days that requires a conviction beyond your feelings and beyond what people are going to think and say.

It calls for faith that believes beyond what you can see, hear and touch!

God showed me through that homework assignment that the foundation hasn't changed, but methods have. If we are to reach a 21st century generation, while embracing change ourselves, some of our methods must change. If our children are to be successful in life, and if we are to be successful, it's going to take doing New Math with a New Math Mind.

I wish I could tell you that those lessons alone changed me, but that wouldn't be true. There's been more than a few situations that have occurred in my life to get me to the place I am now. All of them required doing New Math with a New Math mind.

So much of what we believe in, stand on and hold as our truth will constitute whether we receive a 27 in life or knock it out the park. If we're going to do it lets knock it out of the park.

Sometimes I've said and felt that my life has been so unfair due to all the work and effort that I've had to put into it. Anything worth having requires work. Don't think that it's strange put in the work!

Your life is worth having. It's going to cost you something. Don't let or look at someone else's life and draw conclusions based on assumptions. Do the work, put in the time.

Be willing to look dumb, be willing to sound dumb, be willing to be vulnerable.

All of those are signs when you download an app you don't know anything about. It takes time to learn it. It takes more time to master it. It's nothing wrong with taking the time to read and watch tutorials that will enhance and make you better.

We live in and must contend with the idea of overnight success.

Think of it this way; don't become weary in your well doing or your pursuit for better.

Why? If it took 9 months for you to be born surely in the birthing of who you are to become, don't be so hard on your self in the process. It's going to take doing New Math with a New Math Mind to accomplish it.

Remember this you can eat cake anytime of the year. But there are some occasions that calls for cake.

Birthday, celebrating the day you were born. Anniversary, celebrating the day that you and your spouse began your life's journey together. Retirement, the end of a hard earned career. Thanksgiving, the time when family comes together to give thanks for another year of life and living.

Christmas, the time the world celebrates the birth of our Lord and Savior Jesus. I'm saying it's worth you going in the oven and coming forth at the right time.

There are people waiting to come around you and partake of you in different seasons and times of life. That's what cake does, bring people together. This only happens when you agree and submit to the oven baking class of doing New Math with a New Math Mind.

Chapter Four
"There's Something Incredible Inside You"

While I'm writing this chapter the voice of my mother echoes all over it. All my life that I can remember she would tell me there's something incredible inside you son. To date, I'm still discovering and finding out about all the incredible things inside me. By the way, there are some incredible things inside of you too!

Don't quit, don't throw in the towel yet, it's not over!

No way I can write this book and not make mention of her and the rich contribution she left and deposited into my life. For that I am forever grateful.

Part of my gratefulness is not only writing this playbook and love letter to my son but to commit for the rest of my life to helping others who are in need. That's what the incredible thing inside is for.

Now, my life growing up didn't seem or feel incredible. It felt the opposite. My growing up well that's another book and another time. But I can tell you this, all the bad things that happened and occurred growing up worked overtime to make me feel and not believe that there was something incredible inside me.

Thank God for a mother who was like a broken record playing repeatedly in every season of my life until one day the broken record would take root in my heart.

The wonderful thing about having something incredible inside you is you can bet life is going to deal you enough hands in order to discover it.

Many times, the incredible things will be found due to or out of problems. I know, here we go with that word problems.

Let me explain it this way. Growing up in the 70's as a kid television was the best! A lot of great T.V. shows and a lot of great cartoons. Some of my favorites were the Marvel heroes, particularly the Incredible Hulk.

I loved the cartoon and the T.V. show. What I liked about him then and even now, when he transformed into the Hulk, he was not like any other superhero meaning he became the Hulk out of anger.

I could identify with that because I was angry and upset and I spent a lot of time imagining that I was something else to escape the pain of who I was and my situation in life. Looking at the Hulk's life now, God encourages us about anger but warns us that it should not become sin.

There are things in life that should anger us to change, to be better and to overcome what's trying to overcome us.

When you look at Bruce Banner's life the incredible thing inside him was injected by his father. What seemed to be a curse was a blessing. It's no different with us; God reminds us He knew us before we were formed in our mother's womb and that He knows the thoughts He thinks towards us and to give us an expected end.

All the things I deemed bad where necessary for me to become the man that I am today.

No, all of it didn't feel good, but I'm grateful because I now know, I'm equipped to help someone else know. When I speak of something incredible inside you, I don't mean your social media status or the things from life we use to intoxicate us from truth.

No that's not it. One of the things that makes the Hulk incredible is he's a part of a team that lends to him being better.

Are you apart of a team? If so, do you allow the team to lend to you being and becoming incredible? We all need a team.

Being on and being connected to the right team incubates and grows the incredible things that are inside us.

Some of the greatest athletes and hall of famers are known and talked about year in and year out because of the concept of a team.

Sometimes that team can be many and sometimes it can be just one.

Coaches are great and contribute so much to the vision and destination of the team.

But without the proper Potential Conditioner, many of these great athletes and hall of famers wouldn't be who they are.   Don't you mean Strengthening and Conditioning Coach. No! I mean Potential Conditioner.

I now have my own mentorship mission where I'm the Potential Conditioner that helps rescue and restore the lives of people. There is something incredible in all of us, but it's going to take Potential Conditioners to help us work out, that we may see the results in life.

For the record, there are other Potential Conditioners that have been along my destiny tract and I would like to thank them all! I'm sure there's more to come!

The very thing I was around and exposed to, I now have been doing for the last 25 years! The incredible thing inside those Potential Conditioners ignited the incredible things inside of me. I'm asking you to broaden your perspective and be open to what's happening in every season of your life.

It may be God is giving you snapshots of things to come.

Matthew, I hope this playbook not only help you on your journey but will shine a light on someone else's journey to. I know the word incredible lends to being in a class all by itself. I don't want you to think that you can only be incredible by doing some unimaginable feat or service. No, to the stay at home mom raising the three kids and doing the everyday chores of family there's something incredible in you and to the man who has never been recognized for making sure the park is clean and presentable for the neighborhood children to play there.

There's something incredible inside you. When you begin to look around, you'll notice it's incredible being demonstrated everywhere.

But it takes someone to help reveal it and pull it out of you. When universities recruit players its based-on potential.

The strength and conditioning coaches through a prescription of workouts from the vision of the head coach improves the player so that the potential that the player was recruited on has the best chance to perform at the highest level. Sounds a lot like our everyday lives. There is something incredible inside you and there's a team just for you. If you're not a part of any team, I encourage you to join a team and begin there. Put the time in and listen to the Potential Conditioners and over time, you'll begin to reap the results and rewards you desire in life.

Chapter Five
"It's Time to Make Some Noise"

I love the question that's asked often. When a tree falls in the forest does it make a sound? There have been great debates over whether the tree makes a sound or not. For content of this chapter, I tend to think and believe that things and people, when they fall or fail, it tends to make some noise. I've found that all of us tend to make noise in life.

It's either positive noise or negative noise.

For the most part, when you think of noise, it's referred to and is used as something that's negative and annoying. I want to share and discuss from a viewpoint of noise being the very thing that not only gets positive attention but also causes forward movement in the lives of people.

How I wish I could have understood the noise early on in life.

It could have saved me years and time which are the most precious thing to the living.

When I talk about noise, I speak from living in a place based on your convictions and standards. When done properly, you fight off negative noise and you make noise that beckons for attention. In my teen and college years, there was so much noise that I struggled to navigate my life forward.

The negative noise was a killer not only to my time and some of the best years of my life but to my advancement, growth, vision and destiny.

Vision is so critical! When we choose to or not to make noise, we instead chase after the wrong noise which is devastating.

Noise is an acronym for; **N**egotiate your character and integrity.

Offset your mind, your morals and your maturity.

Isolate your identity.

Sacrifice your position in life. **E**ffort and **E**lection.

This is how we make noise:

> ➤ We fight to keep our character, integrity, mind, morals, maturity, identity, position, election and effort.

I've talked about some of the Potential Conditioners that have made impact in my life throughout this writing, but I want to talk about two

Potential Conditioners reach that's a part of the fabric of who I am today.

I want to acknowledge Al Bass for the positive noise he sparked in my life. He helped me understand that what's happening in your life you control it. I know you're saying that's something you should know. But for a 19-year-old kid, I didn't have that revelation at the time. In life, sometimes you need someone to take you in to help you focus and navigate properly.

Coach Bass was that for me. It was good and intimidating all at the same time! I was able to be up close and he began to mentor me. For me, this was critical because I didn't have it in place in my life. He placed expectations on me like a father would his son! I struggled at first because I'd never had someone to invest in me at this level.

Exposure is critical when hearing the right noise.

Be prepared to be stretched in ways that doesn't always feel good but are necessary. I wish I could say I followed all that was sown into my life from Coach Bass and I reaped the rewards. Not quite. It wouldn't be until years later that I would put a lot of those things into practice.

Because of that relationship and his influence, he helped me get into another college which paid off greatly for me in so many other areas of my life.

He was very instrumental in my life for that season. God was giving me a snapshot of the very thing I would be doing later in life. Never minimize or take for granted the relationships that are placed on your journey.

There was another Potential Conditioner who sparked a noise in my life as a teenager. I want to acknowledge, Howard Ellis. His noise was simply that of spending quality time with me and holding me accountable.

I didn't have an older brother or sister, so he was that for me. He was past that season of his life, but he reached back to help me. He didn't have to do all the things he did. From 8th grade all throughout high school, he invested time, energy and his wisdom.

Looking back at it, one of the passions I have now is directly birthed out of that season, experience and relationship. It helped me to understand the quality of investing time in someone's life.

My passion for my generation and the generation behind me stems from my relationship with Howard. Back home, the community we're from is very small and tight-knit. All the families, graduating classes before you place an expectation on you to excel beyond what they accomplished especially in sports. It's great being a part of that heritage there. It will always be a part of me.

I haven't lived there in years, but the investment from there shows up in my reach in life. Thank you, Howard, for reaching out to this kid from across highway 79.

Many of the experiences I've been blessed to learn and have in my life I've worked hard to pass those along to my children especially my son Matthew. Understanding the sooner, they can begin to make the right noise in life, the better off their lives and the lives of others will be.

Not in any lifetime did I ever think I would be a Potential Conditioner, Mentor and Author, writing about my life to help and encourage my children and others.

I disqualified myself just like many of you who may be reading this. Learn from this writing, if I can overcome the noise I was faced with, so can you.

If not this book, then find someone who can share the positive noise of life so that you can experience life the way it's purposed for you to experience it!

The negative noise will have you thinking and speaking in a manner that it's for everyone except you. Nothing prepares you for life, like being in the fire. I hope when the fires of life come to my son and to you, that you'll have this playbook/ navigational manual that will help you mitigate through the seasons of life. I know what it's like to be lost or in need of direction. It can be frustrating and at times feels hopeless. That's one type of being lost.

Another is having the navigational manual and not using it. Neither is good, but self-inflicted noise causes extra weight to be added to the bench press of life.

Let's face whatever noise that's facing and intimidating us and let's be the noise cancelling headphones controlling that noise!

Matthew this is just the beginning of this journey. And now, more than ever, I understand that there will be intermissions along the journey, but we must never stop. Refresh, renew and even restart if you must but never allow the noise to stop you and make you quit.

I love you Son, Dad.

For More Information Contact Us At:

Email: ucstblaze@gmail.com

Website: harryhickerson.com

UCSTBLAZE